EXPERIMENT WITH SENSES

Written by Monica Byles

Science Consultant: Dr. Nicola Burbidge

Education Consultants: Uschi Spearman and Ruth Bessant

Lerner Publications Company
Minneapolis, Minnesota

All words marked in **bold** can be found in the glossary that begins on page 30.

This edition published in 1994 by:
Lerner Publications Company
241 First Avenue North
Minneapolis, MN 55401

Illustration and design copyright © Two-Can Publishing Ltd, 1992
Text and compilation copyright © Two-Can Publishing Ltd, 1992

First published in Great Britain in 1992 by:
Two-Can Publishing, 346 Old Street, London EC1V 9NQ

Library of Congress Cataloging-in-Publication Data

Byles, Monica.
   Experiment with senses/written by Monica Byles.
     p.   cm.
   "First published in 1992 by Two-Can Pub. Ltd." —T.p. verso. Includes index.
   Summary: Simple experiments demonstrate the five human senses.
   ISBN 0-8225-2455-4
   1. Senses and sensation—Juvenile literature. [1. Senses and sensation—
Experiments. 2. Experiments.] I. Title.
QP434.B95 1994
612.8'078—dc20   92-41110
                                              CIP
                                              AC

Printed in Hong Kong
Bound in the United States of America

1 2 3 4 5 6 99 98 97 96 95 94

ISBN: 0-8225-2455-4

All photographs by Paul Bricknell, except for the following, which are reproduced by permission of: p. 5 (top), ZEFA/R. Iwasaki; p. 5 (bottom), ZEFA/Bob Croxford; p. 7 (top), ZEFA/Wienke; p. 8 (center), ZEFA/A. Thau; p. 9 (top left), ZEFA/ Rauschenbauch; p. 10 (top right), ZEFA/Frans Lanting; p. 11 (top left), Bruce Coleman/ Jane Burton; p. 13 (top right), ZEFA/Jim Brandenburg; p. 16 (bottom), Hutchison/ Dr. Nigel Smith; p. 17 (top), Hutchison/B.D. Drader; p. 19 (top right), Bruce Coleman/ Kim Taylor; p. 19 (center), Bruce Coleman/Bob and Clara Calhoun; p. 20 (top right), Bruce Coleman/Jane Burton; p. 25 (top right), Bruce Coleman/Jon Kenfield; p. 26 (center left), Hutchison/Michael MacIntyre; and pp. 28-29 (center bottom), Guide Dogs for the Blind Association. Cover: ZEFA/Hackenberg. Additional still photographs on pages 4, 5, 6, 7, 11, 12, 13, 14, 15, 16, 18, 20, 23, 24, 25, 27, 28, and 30 are by Toby Maudsley.

Illustrations by Nancy Anderson.

CONTENTS

WHAT ARE THE SENSES?

When you wake up in the morning, do you feel the warmth of your bed, hear the alarm buzzing, see light coming through your window, and sniff for the smell of breakfast cooking?

All of these actions involve your senses. Most people and animals have five senses: sight, hearing, smell, touch, and taste. We all use our senses to receive messages from the world around us. These messages give us useful information, such as whether or not there is danger present, if food is available, or even if other people or animals are friendly.

How many senses would you use if you noticed a kite flying in the sky? Which senses would you use if you picked up a baby duckling calling for its mother? If someone gave you a rose, which senses would tell you it had a sweet fragrance and a thorny stem? Name the senses that could tell you something about a cactus.

Your eyes, ears, tongue, nose, and skin are working all the time, picking up information from the world around you. Even while you sleep, they send signals to your **brain**.

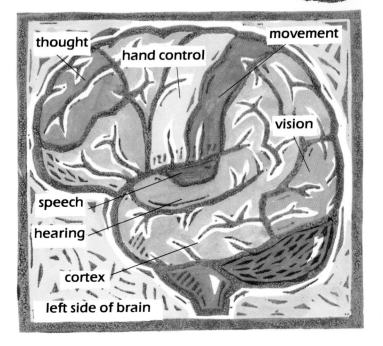

thought

hand control

movement

vision

speech

hearing

cortex

left side of brain

▲ The brain's wrinkly outer layer is called the cortex. Messages from your tongue, eyes, ears, nose, and skin travel along **nerves** to special areas of the cortex. Each area of the cortex is related to a particular sense.

When you look at the strawberries on this page, a message travels from your eyes to your brain. Your brain then sends signals to your mouth, your mouth starts to water, and you may feel hungry.

Messages sent from the left side of your body travel to the right side of your brain—and the left side of your brain receives messages from the right side of your body.

▲ Puppies cannot see when they are born. They use their strong sense of smell to help them find their mother's milk.

▶ Be careful when touching hot things. When you touch something hot, nerve endings in your skin immediately send alarm messages to your brain. Then your brain tells you to pull your skin away from whatever is burning you. This happens automatically, before you have a chance to think about what to do.

SIGHT

Only a small part of your eye can be seen from outside your body. The human eyeball is set back into the skull and is actually the size of a ping-pong ball. Every few seconds, your eyelids blink, covering your eyes with salty liquid. Blinking helps your eyeballs stay moist and removes any dirt and dust that may get in. Your eyebrows keep sweat on your forehead from running into your eyes.

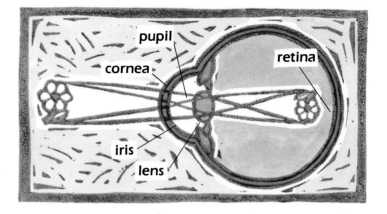

▲ Light **reflected** from an object enters the eye through the **pupil** (the black circle in the center of your eye). The **lens** in your eye **focuses** the image upside down onto light-sensitive cells on the **retina**. The brain turns the image right side up.

▲ A chameleon can swivel its eyes around in their sockets, or even turn one eye forward and the other one backward. Chameleons can see in two different directions at the same time, which helps them watch out for danger.

Your two eyes see things from slightly different angles. The brain joins the two images to make a "3-D" picture for judging depth and distance.

Hawks have very sharp vision, so they can spot prey moving on the ground far below.

A fly's eye is made up of thousands of tiny eyes, each taking in a separate view of an image. The fly's brain then produces a complete picture from all the different images.

Draw pictures with red and green crayons. Then make some cardboard eyeglasses with one red lens and one green lens, using colored cellophane from an art supply store. Look at the pictures with one eye closed, then the other.

Put a variety of objects on a table. Ask a friend to look at the objects for two full minutes, then cover the objects with a cloth. How many things can your friend remember? Now you try. How many things can you remember?

DARK AND BRIGHT

The colored **iris** of the eye controls the amount of light that enters by changing the size of the pupil. In dim light, the pupil gets larger to let more light in. In bright light, the pupil gets smaller.

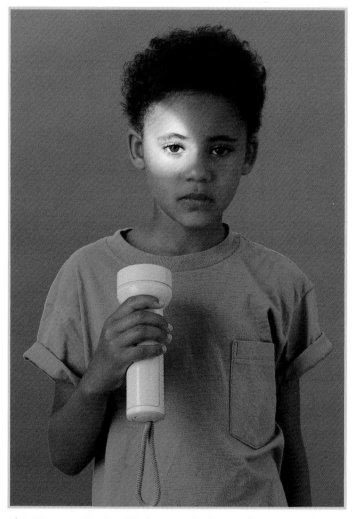

Turn off the light and close the curtains in a room. Point a flashlight so that a little light falls near the face of a friend. Never shine the flashlight directly into someone's eyes. How big is the pupil of your friend's eye? Shine the flashlight closer to the eye. What happens? Look at the other eye. The flashlight is not pointed at this eye and its pupil is still enlarged.

Giraffes have good eyesight. They watch for danger on the flat plains as they nibble leaves from trees.

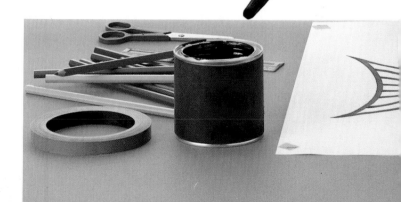

▶ In sunlight, a cat's pupils are narrow slits. At night, the layer of **cells** at the back of a cat's eye acts like a mirror. This layer reflects light to sensitive cells at the front of the eye so that extra light signals reach the brain. Cats can see much better in dim light than people can.

Draw or paint a shape with thick black lines on plain white paper. Stare hard at it for at least one minute. Now close your eyes tightly. What do you see? For a little while, your brain will "remember" the shape. But the black parts of the picture will look white, and the white parts will look black.

SMELL

Your nose is very sensitive. It can detect many thousands of different smells. You also use it to take in air for your lungs to breathe in and out.

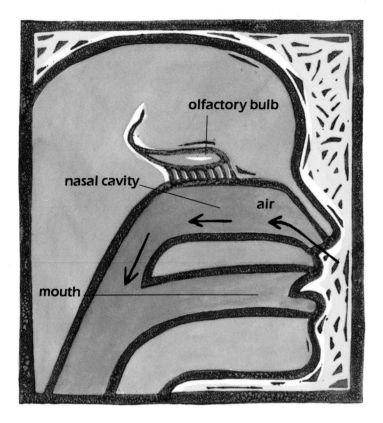

When you breathe, air is sucked into your nose. Air passes over the **olfactory bulb**, where tiny hairs trap any dirt and dust. When the air reaches the olfactory bulb, it passes over nerves that send signals to the brain. The brain interprets the signals as smells.

How well can you smell? Blindfold a friend and ask her to identify a number of foods by sniffing them. You could ask her to smell orange juice, garlic, ginger, mustard, and flour. Can she tell them apart? Mix two of the substances together. Can she still tell

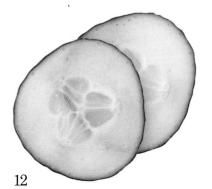

what she is smelling? Other things you could include in the smell test are slices of cucumber, lemon, cheese, carrots, or cinnamon.

Members of the dog family, such as these Arctic wolves, have noses many times more sensitive than human noses. This is partly because their noses are much longer and larger. Dogs use their sense of smell to find food and to distinguish between friends and enemies.

SCENT

Some people use their sense of smell at work. Perfume makers can identify up to 10,000 different **scents.** They try to figure out which scents people will like, and which they won't. They mix different scents together until they make a perfume they think smells just right.

Bath oil, stationery, tissues, and soaps often have nice-smelling scents added to them to make them more appealing. Many scents are made artificially (with chemicals in a laboratory). Most perfumes are created from natural sources such as lavender, rose, and jasmine petals. Sometimes scents are used to keep things away. Moths stay away from clothes stored with smelly moth balls.

Have you ever noticed how bad food smells when it begins to spoil? Maybe you have seen signs of mold, too. Both mold and bad smells are nature's way of warning you not to eat food that could make you sick. **Bacteria** start to grow on old food and break it down, releasing the bad odor.

Make a scratch-and-sniff card. Draw a shape on a piece of construction paper and glue herbs, spices, or flowers to different parts of the drawing. You can make it look very colorful. Can your friends tell by sniffing exactly what you used? You can use the card for a special friend's birthday.

TASTE

Your tongue helps you to speak. It also allows you to taste and eat food. It is a muscle that can curl in many directions. The tongue sorts and shapes food as you chew and swallow.

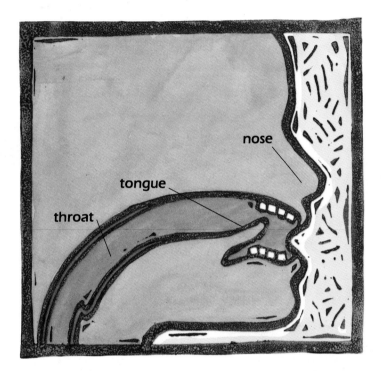

Do you like eating seafood like these mussels? All over the world, people enjoy eating a huge variety of different foods. Some Aborigines in Australia love to eat fat, white whichetty grubs, fresh or toasted over a fire. Other delicacies that some people eat include dried seaweed, frog's legs, snails, snakes, and chocolate-covered grasshoppers. Which food tastes best to you?

Sticks of edible clay, such as these, are eaten by some people in Nigeria. The clay adds a valuable source of calcium to their diet. Calcium is a **mineral** used by our bodies to make bones and blood, and to clot blood when we cut ourselves. People need to eat a balanced mixture of minerals, fats, vitamins, fiber, and carbohydrates to stay healthy.

How many crackers can you eat in one minute without drinking anything? To keep you from choking, **saliva** comes out of **glands** in your tongue and cheeks and mixes with food in your mouth to make a smooth, wet paste. Saliva also starts to digest, or break down, the food.

Smells affect the way things taste. Ask a friend to shut her eyes. Hold an onion to her nose, but have her bite into an apple. She will think she is eating an onion because that is what she smells.

SWEET AND SOUR

Your tongue recognizes four basic tastes. These tastes combine with thousands of smells to make up all the taste sensations you experience when you eat and drink.

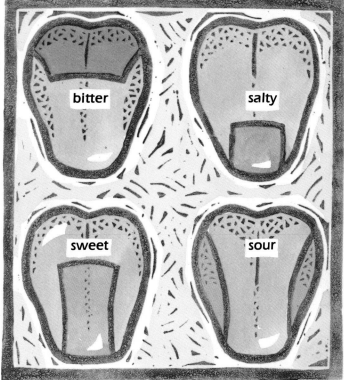

bitter   salty

sweet   sour

▲ Your tongue is covered with about 3,000 taste buds. These are tiny openings in the tongue's surface, lined with taste-sensitive cells. There are four main types of taste: sweet, bitter, salty, and sour. Groups of buds are better at sensing one type of taste than another. Messages pass from the buds along nerves to the part of your brain that identifies taste.

▼ How food or drink tastes is often influenced by its color. Put drops of different food coloring into glasses of juice. Can your friends identify each fruity flavor, or are they confused by the coloring?

▶ Toads can flick their tongues out and back again in one-tenth of a second.

▲ Hummingbirds have very long, thin tongues and beaks to reach the sugary nectar in flowers. Hummingbirds eat things much sweeter than people eat. Sugar provides the energy they need to keep their hearts and wings beating rapidly.

TOUCH

Sensors (sensitive nerve endings) in your skin constantly give your brain information. Sometimes these sensors tell you that you are too hot or too cold. They also tell you if something is wet, dry, soft, or prickly.

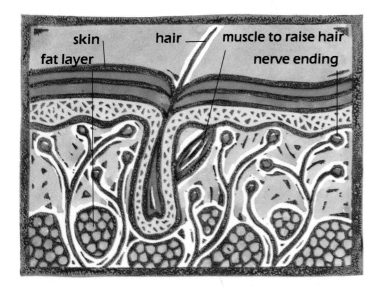

skin
fat layer
hair
muscle to raise hair
nerve ending

▲ Flies trigger touch-sensitive hairs on Venus flytraps. Then the plant's leaves trap flies for the plant to digest.

▲ Skin is an organ that covers your whole body. Skin stretches so that when you move or grow, it moves and grows with you. Your skin is constantly being replaced. Millions of skin cells are lost from your body every day.

Skin is oily, which helps keep you water-proof. When you are hot, glands in your skin produce sweat. Air dries the sweat and cools you off. When you are chilly, your hairs rise to trap a layer of warm air next to your skin. All over your skin, nerve endings are at work, sending messages to your brain.

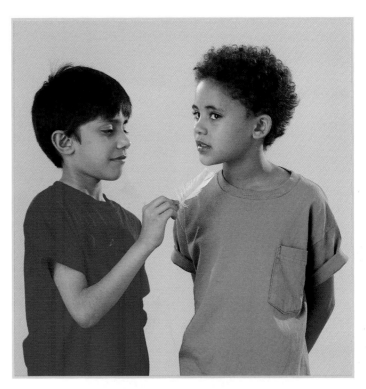

▲ Tickle a friend with a feather. Which areas of skin are the most sensitive?

▼ Every single person in the world has a unique pattern of tiny ridges on his or her fingertips. The police use fingerprints to help track down criminals. Make fingerprints of your family and friends. Press each fingertip on a stamp pad, then onto paper. With a magnifying glass, examine the fingerprints to see how they are different from each other.

▲ The color of your skin depends on how much **melanin** it contains. Melanin is a pigment that helps protect the skin against sunburn. People with fair skin have little melanin. After a few days in the sun, their skin produces more melanin and develops a tan. People with darker skin have a lot of melanin.

HOT AND COLD

How sensitive are you? Lightly touch various areas of your skin with the points of a pair of tweezers. Which areas can sense both points? Draw a picture of your body. Label the areas of your body that can feel only one point and those that can feel two points.

Nerve endings in some parts of the body are much less sensitive to hot and cold than others. Do you dip your toes into the bathtub or swimming pool to check the water temperature before you get in?

Make a hole in the side of a box. Ask your friends, one by one, to put their hands into the box and to identify the objects inside by touch alone. You can use objects with different **textures**, such as a sponge, an orange, raisins, a hairbrush, a soft toy, or a leaf. How many things can they identify?

See how cold things affect your sense of touch. Put your fingers in a bowl of *melting* ice cubes for about 30 seconds. Now touch something very soft, and then something prickly. What do you feel? The cold of the ice cubes numbs your nerve endings so they do not send accurate signals to your brain.

Do not touch ice straight from the freezer — it could harm your skin.

HEARING

What can you hear around you? Listen to the sounds your fingertips make when you rub them together next to your ear. What is the most quiet sound you can hear?

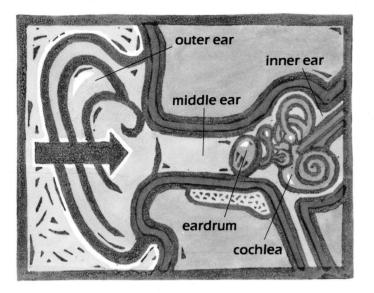

outer ear

inner ear

middle ear

eardrum

cochlea

▲ The ear is made up of three parts. Sound travels through the air to the cup-shaped outer ear. Then it travels into the middle ear. Here, the sound **vibrates** a thin **membrane** called the eardrum. Tiny bones in the middle ear vibrate, together with liquid in the **cochlea,** which is part of the inner ear. Nerves translate the vibrations into signals to the brain. The brain interprets these signals as sounds.

▼ Place some uncooked rice or small pieces of candy on a drum. Hold a cookie sheet above the drum and hit it. Sound will travel through the air, causing the drum to vibrate like an eardrum and shake the rice or candy.

Sound can travel through solid objects like walls or the ground. What can you hear if you put your ear to the ground?

Dolphins communicate by sending high-pitched clicks through the water. They judge distances by the time it takes the echoes to return.

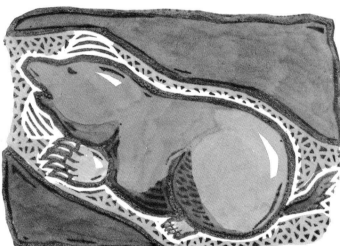

To avoid running into each other, moles bump their heads against the sides of their tunnels. This sends vibrations through the earth, warning other moles to stay away.

Ask an adult to pierce a hole in the end of two plastic cups or tin cans. Push about six feet of string through the holes and knot the ends so the string won't slip through. Have a friend hold one cup and then walk away to pull the string tight. Ask the friend to put the cup to his or her ear. Speak into your cup. Your voice sends sound traveling along the string of your special telephone.

LOUD AND SOFT

Sounds are often pleasant, but some can harm your ears. At a party or concert, the noise may be so loud that you later hear ringing in your ears. If so, your ears have suffered temporary damage.

Large machinery such as bulldozers, or smaller equipment such as jackhammers can produce deafening sound levels. In many countries, workers are required by law to wear protective earguards if sound levels are too loud. Too much noise in the environment is called noise pollution.

People and animals all hear sounds a little differently. Your friend's favorite music may sound terrible to you. Some sounds are too high or too low for people to hear. Sounds from dog whistles, and some bird, insect, and bat noises are too high. We feel very low sounds as rumbling vibrations.

▲ Next time you see a vehicle with a wailing siren, listen closely to the sound it makes. The sound changes as the vehicle approaches, then passes by you. You can hear the same effect by asking a friend to ride past you on a bike while blowing a whistle. The sound itself does not change—only the way that your own ears receive the sound changes.

Many people are born without the full use of one or more senses, or they lose them later through accident or illness. Their other senses may become sharper as a result.

▲ Many people wear contact lenses or glasses. The extra lenses change the way light hits the eyes. Without contact lenses or glasses, nearsighted eyes cannot focus on distant objects, and farsighted eyes cannot focus on near objects.

The Braille System

CELL

A B C D E

F G H I J

K L M N O

P Q R S T

U V X Y Z

▲ In 1829, a blind man in France named Louis Braille developed a system of reading and writing using patterns of raised dots, which are read with the fingertips. Braille is used all over the world. Language systems for people who are deaf involve signing with the hands, reading lips, and reading and writing.

As people grow older, their sense organs may become less sensitive. They may need eyeglasses or a hearing aid.

Guide dogs are trained to be the eyes of their blind owners. Each guide dog wears a harness, which is held by the owner. The dogs signal danger or whether it is safe to cross the street.

GLOSSARY

bacteria: very tiny forms of life that live in air, water, soil, and in and on plants and animals. Some bacteria cause disease.

brain: the organ in the skull that receives information from the body's other organs, stores memory, makes decisions, and causes the muscles to move

cells: tiny pieces of living matter from which all living things are made

cochlea (KO-klee-uh): a tube in the ear filled with fluid and lined with tiny hairs. Sound vibrations move the hairs, which send hearing signals to the brain.

focus: to adjust a lens (such as the eye) in order to make an image clear

glands: organs in the body, such as sweat glands in the skin or tear glands near the eyes, that either produce chemical substances or help get rid of waste products from the body

iris: the part of the eye that has color. The iris controls the amount of light that enters the eye by changing the size of the pupil.

lens: the part of the eye located behind the iris that focuses light on the retina

melanin: the substance in skin that gives it color. People with dark skin have a lot of melanin, while people with lighter skin have very little melanin.

membrane: a very thin layer of skin or body tissue that joins or covers parts of a plant or animal

nerves: long, thin cells that run between organs all over the body. Sensory nerves carry messages from the sense organs to the brain. Motor nerves carry messages from the brain to the muscles, telling them what to do.

olfactory bulb: the organ inside the nose that contains sensory nerves. The brain interprets signals from these nerves as smells.

pupil: the small, round, black opening in the middle of the front of the eye. Light enters the eye through the pupil.

reflect: to bounce light off a surface

retina: the light-sensitive area at the back of the eye that sends light signals to the brain

saliva: the liquid produced by glands in the cheeks and tongue that helps people mash food up and swallow it more easily. Saliva also contains a chemical that starts to break the food down.

texture: the feeling of an object's surface, such as the softness of a furry kitten or the roughness of scratchy sandpaper

vibrate: to quiver rapidly, back and forth. Sound travels as vibrations. A strong vibration can be powerful enough to knock down a building.

INDEX